Macbeth
Study Guide

by Michael S. Gilleland

Limited permission to reproduce this study guide

Purchase of this book entitles an individual teacher to reproduce pages for use in the classroom or home. Multiple teachers may not reproduce pages from the same study guide.

Macbeth Study Guide
A Progeny Press Study Guide
by Michael S. Gilleland
with Andrew Clausen, Calvin Roso, Rebecca Gilleland

Copyright © 2000 Progeny Press
All rights reserved.

Reproduction or translation of any part of this work beyond that permitted by Section 107 or 108 of the 1976 United States Copyright Act without the written permission of the copyright owner is unlawful. Requests for permission or other information should be addressed to Reprint Permissions, Progeny Press, P.O. Box 100, Fall Creek, WI 54742-0100.

Printed in the United States of America.

ISBN: 1-58609-170-0

Table of Contents

Note to Instructor 1

Synopsis 2

Background Information 4

About the Author 5

Suggestions for Pre-reading Activities 6

Act I 7

Act II 14

Act III 21

Act IV 29

Act V 34

Overview 41

Writing Projects 47

Answer Key 49

Suggestions for Further Reading 60

How to Use This Guide

In preparing study guides, we have attempted to divide the reading of each book into manageable sections. For the shorter books at lower grade levels, this sometimes means examining the story as a whole. More often, however, the readings are divided into chapters or groups of chapters of similar length or theme. Students should read the chapters indicated and complete that section of the study guide before continuing with the reading.

The study guide provides vocabulary exercises and questions corresponding to each section of reading. Vocabulary exercises for a section are best done before that section is read. However, when vocabulary exercises refer to the context of a word, exercises may be done during or after the reading.

The questions found in each section of the guide generally progress from basic story comprehension to questions dealing with themes, characters, and applications to the students' lives. But the most important thing to keep in mind when using this study guide is that it is simply a *guide*. Although we feel the study guide is most effective when used in its entirety, you may find that individual questions may not be pertinent to your students. It is perfectly acceptable to choose exercises based on the ability of your students or to choose exercises that accentuate or act as a springboard to your own lessons.

If you find that your students are having trouble keeping up in the study guide, or are very resistant to reading the book and using the study guide, you may try giving the students more time to complete lessons either by literally allowing more time or by having the students answer fewer questions in each lesson.

Bible passages used and referred to in this guide are generally from the New International Version of the Bible. We have indicated where other versions are used.

Macbeth Study Guide

Note to Instructor

A first encounter with Shakespeare can be a challenging experience for high school students. The spelling is often nonstandard, the vocabulary is difficult and archaic, and the cadence and structure are unfamiliar. These barriers to understanding the story could cause a student to become frustrated with the literature and give up. To enhance the student's appreciation and understanding of *Macbeth,* we urge instructors to carefully consider the edition your students will read. We suggest selecting an annotated edition that uses standard spelling but retains the original sentence structure. We recommend *The New Folger Library Shakespeare* editions.

In addition, since Shakespeare wrote his plays to be performed and not merely read, we recommend the use of video or audio recordings of *Macbeth* as part of the learning process. These may be available through your local library. We advise letting students watch or listen to the play before actually reading it. This helps familiarize the students with the story and the language and makes in-depth study of the text easier. Note that every performance is an interpretation, however, and so may not match perfectly with the text.

Synopsis

A day of storm and battle is coming to a close, and Duncan, king of Scotland awaits news of the conflict. A bloody man appears and tells him that against all odds, the rebel Macdonwald, the traitor Thane of Cawdor, and the king of Norway have been defeated by Duncan's captains, Macbeth and Banquo. Duncan orders the Thane of Cawdor executed and tells his men to go bestow the title on Macbeth.

Macbeth and Banquo, returning from the battle, come upon three witches who greet Macbeth as thane of Glamis, thane of Cawdor, and king to be. Banquo asks whether they have such complimentary greetings for him. They call him "Lesser than Macbeth and greater," and tell him that he will father kings. Then the witches vanish.

Not certain what to make of this, Macbeth and Banquo are soon joined by Ross, who greets them in the king's name and names Macbeth Thane of Cawdor. This news, in fulfillment of the witches' statement seems to awaken within Macbeth a long-dead desire for the throne. Hardly daring to admit his own thoughts to himself, he writes to tell his wife of these events.

Lady Macbeth has fewer qualms than her husband and goes into near-ecstasy at the thought of taking the throne. When she learns the king is coming to their castle for a night, she and Macbeth plot Duncan's death.

In the dead of night Macbeth and his wife stab the king and leave the bloody daggers with his attendants. When the king is discovered the next morning, Macbeth kills the attendants in a "fit of rage." Realizing that they no longer know who to trust, and that whoever killed their father may well be after them next, Duncan's sons Malcolm and Donalbain flee to England and Ireland. Immediately, the lords assume they were behind the king's death and name Macbeth king.

Not all are convinced of the wisdom of this, however. Banquo is keenly aware that the king has died in Macbeth's home shortly after Macbeth heard a prediction that he will be king. Macduff also doubts the innocence of Macbeth and, though he does not voice his thoughts, he refuses to attend Macbeth's coronation.

Now that Macbeth is king, however, he remembers the prediction of the witches: Banquo's son will reign, not his. He hires men to kill Banquo and his son

Fleance, but they acheive only partial success—Fleance escapes. At the banquet held in his honor that evening, Macbeth sees the ghost of Banquo, and in shouting at it perhaps reveals more than he intends to the gathered lords. He also begins to fear Macduff and determines to visit the witches again.

The witches call forth three apparitions, who tell Macbeth that he must beware Macduff, but "no one of woman born" can harm him, and he will never be defeated until Birnam Wood comes to Dunsinane. Heartened by these predictions, Macbeth demands to know whether Banquo's descendents will, indeed, rule after him. The witches show him a seemingly endless line of kings descending from Banquo. Angry, Macbeth decides to remove his last available irritant by killing Macduff. As he departs, however, he is told Macduff has fled to Malcolm in England. Now enraged, Macbeth vows from this point forward to immediately follow his first impulses, and he vents his fury by slaughtering everyone he can find in Macduff's castle—Macduff's wife, children, and servants.

In England, Macduff has found Malcolm, but Malcolm is distrustful of him. As they form a tentative alliance, word arrives of the slaughter of Macduff's family. Macduff vows vengeance on Macbeth. Heartened by reports of rebellion against Macbeth and the offer of support and troops from England, Malcolm and Macduff make plans to return to Scotland and reclaim the throne.

Things have not been going well for Macbeth and Lady Macbeth. The rebellions are taking their toll, and Lady Macbeth is restless in her mind. Her gentlewoman and a doctor observe her sleepwalking, speaking of the murders and clearly disturbed. Macbeth appears manic, thrown this way and that by his whims, alternating between supreme self-confidence in the predictions of the witches and fury that things are not as he wishes them. The death of Lady Macbeth seems to affect him little beyond a morose discussion about the meaning of life.

Things really begin to fall apart as Malcolm's troops advance to Dunsinane and are joined by the lords of Scotland. When the troops pause at Birnam Wood, Malcolm orders his men to cut down and carry branches of the wood to confuse reports of their numbers. As this movement of the Wood pours toward Dunsinane, Macbeth realizes that the predictions he relied on have become a two-edged sword. Maddened by the desertion of his subjects and faced with an apparent trap, he clings to, almost revels in, the prediction that no one born of woman can harm him. But in the end, even this fails Macbeth.

Background Information

Shakespeare got many of the ideas for his plays from European history, and *Macbeth* is no different. In Raphael Holinshed's histories of Scotland, Shakespeare found a story of betrayal and murder with hints of the supernatural. As was often true of Shakespeare, however, he did not let historical facts deter him from creating a masterful play to please his audience, and he freely reinterpreted the events and characters to match them to his audience.

His audience for this play was ruled by a new king, James I of England. Queen Elizabeth died in 1603 and was followed by James VI of Scotland, who became James I of England. James was son of Mary Queen of Scots, and he took the throne of Scotland when she abdicated in 1567—James was one year old. His reign and life were filled with intrigue between Catholics and Protestants, including his being kidnapped by Protestants while he was king of Scotland and a bombing plot by Catholics shortly after he ascended the English throne. These events led to a certain degree of paranoia. James also strongly believed in the divine right of kings, was vain and headstrong, and held little regard for the English Parliament, attitudes that did not endear him to the English aristocracy.

Probably James' most lasting act was commissioning a new translation of the Bible, the King James Authorized Version, still commonly used today. He was a firm believer in witches and demons, writing works of his own on the topic and blaming them for various events in his life.

Within this framework, Shakespeare wrote *Macbeth*, taking an historical occurrence and fitting it to the life and prejudices of James, his new patron. The people and locations Shakespeare used were real; in fact, King James was a decendent of Banquo, who was prophecied to father a long line of kings. Shakespeare blended facts and the preferences of his audience to create a play that still intrigues and haunts us.

About the Author

William Shakespeare was born in Stratford-upon-Avon in April 1564. Traditionally his birth is celebrated on April 23. Little is known for certain about his life. He was one of eight children born to John Shakespeare, a merchant of some standing in Stratford-upon-Avon. William probably had some formal schooling but never attended college. At age 18, Shakespeare married Anne Hathaway, who was eight years older than he. They had a daughter, named Susanna, on May 26, 1583. In 1585 the Shakespeares had twins—a boy, Hamnet, and a girl, Judith. Hamnet died at age 11.

By 1592 Shakespeare had moved to London to work as an actor and a playwright. He had little success with acting, but continued to write. One dramatist, Robert Greene, called Shakespeare "an upstart crow, beautified with our feathers." Eventually Shakespeare became a large shareholder and playwright for the acting troupe The Lord Chamberlain's Men. In 1599 the acting company built and occupied the Globe Theatre in Southwark.

Shakespeare's plays can be categorized into four types: historical plays, comedies, tragedies, and romances. Besides writing 37 plays, he wrote 154 sonnets.

Shakespeare died on April 23, 1616, and was buried in Holy Trinity Church, Stratford.

Macbeth Study Guide

Suggestions for Pre-reading Activities

- Read 1 Samuel 16:1–13, 18:1–10, 24:1–22, 26:1–25, 31:1–7, 2 Samuel 2:1–4. Write a 1–2 page summary of what occurs in these passages.

- Prepare an oral or written report on the background and reign of King James I of England.

- *Map Work:* Make a map of Scotland, showing the locations of Cumberland, Cawdor, Glamis, Forres, Inverness, Scone, Colmekill (Iona), Birnam Wood, Dunsinane.

- The desire for power and the use of power will play a large role in Macbeth. Choose a national or world leader from the last 100 years who was known for his (or her) desire for or use of power and write a report on that person's effect on his time and surroundings.

- Watch a video on Scotland, particularly on the Highlands and the monuments or castles of Scotland.

- Read Machiavelli's *The Prince* and compare its pure pragmatism and lack of scruples to Macbeth and Lady Macbeth.

- *As you read:* As you go through the play, copy your favorite phrases or passages into a notebook. They may be important to you for what they mean, for the word picture they give, for the way they sound, or for some other reason. Make a brief note about why you choose each phrase.

Macbeth Study Guide

Act I

Vocabulary:

Write the letter of the definition on the right in the blank next the the word it defines.

___ 1. plight   a. relating to the body
___ 2. vantage   b. pay out, spread around
___ 3. curb   c. matchless, unequaled
___ 4. disburse   d. predicament, situation
___ 5. inhabitant   e. deposit, pledge, downpayment
___ 6. corporal   f. triviality
___ 7. earnest   g. reward, compensation
___ 8. trifle   h. superior position
___ 9. recompense   i. restrain, repress
___ 10. peerless   j. resident, dweller

Scrambled Quotation:

The following words are a quotation from Act I. See if you can unscramble the quotation. Next to the quotation, write the name of the person speaking and the act and scene in which it is found.

in no face art There's the construction to find the mind's.

© 2000 Progeny Press

General Questions:

1. Who turns the tide of the battle for King Duncan?

2. Who delivers some prophecies to Macbeth and Banquo, and what are the prophecies?

3. To whom is Macbeth referring in scene iv, when he says "The Prince of Cumberland! That is a step/ On which I must fall down or else o'erleap"? What does his statement mean?

4. At the end of Act I, what have Macbeth and his Lady planned? Explain their plans.

Analysis:

5. The opening scene in Macbeth is possibly the strangest opening in all of Shakespeare's plays. What tone does it set for play? How does the first scene affect your expectations for the play?

6. In scene iv, Duncan says of the former Thane of Cawdor, "There's no art/ To find the mind's construction in the face./ He was a gentleman on whom I built/ An absolute trust." Immediately after this statement, Macbeth enters. What is ironic about Macbeth appearing after Duncan says this?

7. This play makes much of contrasting what is natural with what is unnatural. Banquo calls attention to this in the case of the three Weird Sisters:

> *Banquo* What are these,
> So withered, and so wild in their attire,
> That look not like th' inhabitants o' th' earth
> And yet are on 't?—Live you? Or are you aught
> That man may question? You seem to understand me
> By each at once her choppy finger laying
> Upon her skinny lips. You should be women,
> And yet your beards forbid me to interpret
> That you are so.
> (scene iii, lines 40–49)

The witches are not quite human, not quite spirit; they are female, but not really women—they are distinctly unnatural. Find another instance of someone acting unnaturally in Act I and describe it. Does the unnaturalness appear good or bad?

Macbeth Study Guide

Character Study:
8. Pick one or two of the following characters from the play and describe their qualities, using examples from Act I. What kind of people are they? What are their strengths and weaknesses?

        Macbeth   Lady Macbeth
        Duncan   Banquo

9. An *aside* is when a sentence or two is spoken in an undertone by one character to the audience or to another character. It is understood that the other characters on stage do not hear the aside. Asides help the audience know a character better by allowing that character to privately express feelings, opinions, and reactions. In all of Act I, who is the only character to speak in asides or to instigate aside exchanges between two characters? Act I, scene iii, has more asides than the rest of the play combined. Considering that asides are, in essence, secrets or whispers kept from the rest of the characters, and considering who is speaking the asides, what does this imply about that character?

Foreshadowing:
10. *Foreshadowing* is a literary device by which the author hints at events to come later in the play. At the end of scene i, the three witches chant together "Fair is foul, and foul is fair." As you look at Act I, what are the witches foreshadowing? What do you think this foreshadows for the rest of the play?

11. The pacing of Macbeth is rapid-fire—there are many drastic scene changes, and events move very quickly. How do you think this rapid change of circumstances affects Macbeth's ability to sort through events and come to decisions? Consider Proverbs 19:2.

12. A *soliloquy* is a speech a character makes when alone on stage, generally to provide background information or express what she is thinking. In Lady Macbeth's soliloquy at the start of scene v, from what "weaknesses" does she say Macbeth suffers? To what "illness" do you think Lady Macbeth refers when she says Macbeth is "not without ambition, but without/ The illness should attend it"?

13. When does Macbeth first consider murdering the king? What does this tell us about Macbeth?

14. *Contrast* is a stylistic device in which different things are held up in opposition to each other. For example, a rural setting may be contrasted with, or held up as an opposing image to, an urban setting. An author may also create stylistic contrast by using long and short sentences or short-worded, staccato passages next to longer, more fluid passages.

    Explain the contrast in scene vi between Duncan's and Banquo's description of the castle and the plans being laid within the castle, or the contrast between Duncan's statements to Lady Macbeth and her plans for him.

Macbeth Study Guide

Dig Deeper:

15. Read 1 Samuel 26. What is Abishai's reaction to David's opportunity in the camp? Does David see it the same way as Abishai? How do their reactions compare to Macbeth's and Lady Macbeth's ideas about Duncan visiting their castle?

16. To how many people does Macbeth confide his thoughts, desires, and plans? From how many people does he seek advice? Do you think this affects his plans at the end of Act I? Read Proverbs 11:14, 12:15, 19:20, 20:18. How might these verses have affected Macbeth's actions? How can you use these verses in your life?

17. Toward the end of scene vii, Lady Macbeth accuses Macbeth of unmanliness. Compare Lady Macbeth's definition of manliness with the definition found in Proverbs 3 and 4.

18. In his soliloquy at the beginning of scene vii, Macbeth reviews his reasons against murdering Duncan. Summarize this soliloquy. What does this reveal about Macbeth?

19. Read Galatians 5:7–8 and Colossians 2:6–8. How do these verses relate to what Macbeth is doing in this Act? Why do you think it is so easy for people to discard what they know is right? How can you avoid this?

Extra Activities:

- In Act I, scene iii, Banquo warns Macbeth, "Oftentimes, to win us to our harm,/ The instruments of darkness tell us truths,/ Win us with honest trifles, to betray 's/ In deepest consequence." Write a one-page essay discussing the meaning of these statements and how they explain and warn against temptation.

- Research King James I of England and write a one- or two-page paper summarizing James' life. Examine whether Shakespeare wrote actions or events into Act I of Macbeth to particularly appeal to the king or to reflect events in his life.

- Paint a watercolor or draw a colored pencil rendition of Macbeth's castle at Inverness, drawing inspiration from the descriptions of Duncan and Banquo from Act I, scene vi.

- Have one person act out a portion or all of the dialogue between Macbeth and Lady Macbeth in Act I, scene vii. Note how voice, tone, and pacing must change to depict the character and communicate him or her to the audience. If possible, have several students do this exercise. Other scenes may be chosen.

- Have two students act out the above dialogue or another, each taking the part of a character. Then have the students act out the same scene but exchange characters.

Act II

Vocabulary:

Circle the letter of the definition that most closely matches the underlined words below.

1. "When we can <u>entreat</u> an hour to serve, we should spend it in some words upon that business."

    a. ask, beg, find   b. place of relaxation   c. crave, long for

2. "So I lose none in seeking to <u>augment</u> [my honor], but still keep my bosom franchised and allegiance clear."

    a. drill, make a hole   b. color, make bright   c. to add to, increase

3. "I see thee yet, in form as <u>palpable</u> as this which now I draw."

    a. squished, mushy   b. relating to the hand   c. tangible, clear, definite

4. "The doors are open, and the <u>surfeited</u> grooms do mock their charge with their snores."

    a. glutted, overfilled   b. sleeping, lazy   c. ugly, repulsive

5. "Sleep . . . sore labor's bath, <u>balm</u> of hurt minds, great nature's second course, chief nourisher in life's feast."

    a. warm, sunny   b. salve, sedative   c. pain, soreness

6. "Faith, here's an <u>equivocator</u> that could swear in both the scales against either scale, who committed treason enough."

    a. mathematician   b. lawyer for the government   c. one who distorts truth or uses double meaning

Macbeth Study Guide

7. "Most <u>sacrilegious</u> murder hath broken ope the Lord's anointed temple and stole thence the life o' th' building."

    a. bloody, gruesome   b. violation or destruction   c. untimely, inconvenient of something sacred

8. "From this instant there's nothing serious in mortality. All is but toys. <u>Renown</u> and grace is dead."

    a. glory, distinction   b. wisdom, knowledge   c. ability to recover

Scrambled Quotation:

The following words are a quotation from Act II. See if you can unscramble the quotation. Next to the quotation, write the name of the person speaking and the act and scene in which it is found.

    cursed repose in me restrain the powers
    nature gives to thoughts that in Merciful way

General Questions:

1. What time is it at the beginning of Act II, scene i? How does that fit with what happens in Act II?

2. What object does Macbeth imagine he sees before him, leading him to Duncan's room?

3. Shakespeare is known for his use of comic relief in his plays. Which character in Act II is used as comic relief?

4. What does the porter imagine himself to be when he answers the knocking at the south gate?

5. Who does Macbeth kill in this act?

6. What do Duncan's sons do at his death? What does this cause people to believe?

Analysis:

7. What word does Macbeth find that he cannot say? Why do you think he cannot say this?

8. A *foil* is a person who, by being opposite or very different from another person, brings out and makes more apparent character traits that are in the other. For example, a passive character might be used to foil an aggressive character to make the aggression more stark. How does Shakespeare use Banquo as a foil to Macbeth in Act II, scene i?

9. Paraphrase the following exchange between Macbeth and Banquo:

> *Macbeth* If you shall cleave to my consent, when 'tis,
> It shall be honor for you.
>
> *Banquo* So I lose none
> In seeking to augment it, but still keep
> My bosom franchised and allegiance clear,
> I shall be counseled.
> (scene i, lines 34–39)

What is Macbeth trying to do? How could Banquo's response mean trouble for Macbeth?

10. *Pathetic fallacy* is a literary term attributing human traits and emotion to nature (pathetic—feelings/emotions; fallacy—false notion; false notion of feelings). It is closely affiliated with *personification,* attributing human traits or emotions to a nonhuman creature or object. "The sun hid its face" is an example of personification. Although pathetic fallacy is sometimes used interchangeably with personification, pathetic fallacy is generally considered to be more sweeping in its scope—several events of personification connected together or several events that, viewed together, give human traits to nature in general. In scene iii, lines 61–69, Lennox's description of the night is an example of pathetic fallacy:

> *Lennox:* The night has been unruly. Where we lay,
> Our chimneys were blown down and, as they say,
> Lamentings heard i' th' air, strange screams of death,
> And prophesying, with accents terrible,
> Of dire combustion and confused events
> New hatched to th' woeful time. The obscure bird
> Clamored the livelong night. Some say the earth
> Was feverous and did shake.

List two examples of personification and one example of pathetic fallacy from Act II.

11. In Act II, in what ways (besides murder) does Macbeth's behavior become unheroic, even unmanly? What do you think causes this behavior?

12. The pacing in Act I was swift and the scenes changed often. In Act II there are half as many scenes, yet the pacing seems at least as fast. How does Shakespeare give a feeling almost of frenzy to the early dialogue between Macbeth and Lady Macbeth early in Act II, scene ii?

13. *Understatement* emphasizes or draws attention to something by saying it is less than it truly is. *Hyperbole* (hi PER bo lee) is the opposite, it is dramatic exaggeration. For example, the statement "Getting old is better than the alternative," is understatement; "when she took the sliver out it felt like she was cutting off my hand" is hyperbole. Both generally are used for irony or humor, though they are also used to express strong feeling, and to be effective the reader must know the true state of things. Find one example each of understatement and hyperbole in Act II, scene iii. Describe why the examples are understatement or hyperbole and whether the effect is ironic, humorous, or dramatic.

14. Given Macbeth's sparse speech earlier in Act II, scene iii, why do you think he is so dramatic in his statements after Macduff finds the king? Why do you think Lady Macbeth seems to faint?

15. *Anaphora* is the repetition of a word or phrase, usually at the beginning or end of a sentence or paragraph. It is used to draw attention to an idea or to unify ideas within the text. Find an example of anaphora in Act II, scene ii. What do you think is its significance?

16. What do Macduff's statements and actions at the end of Act II imply about his feelings toward Macbeth and recent events?

Dig Deeper:

17. What two reasons do Malcolm and Donalbain give for fleeing the castle? Do you think this was wise? What would you do in their situation?

18. In Act II, scene ii, Lady Macbeth says, referring to Duncan's murder, "A little water clears us of this deed." Read Psalm 51:1–7, 16, 17. What truly clears us of sin?

19. In the discussion between Lennox and the old man at the beginning of Act II, scene iv, they list three occurrences that are against nature. What are these occurrences and what is unnatural about them? How might these occurrences represent or be metaphors for the events of this Act?

20. At the end of Act II, scene ii, Macbeth exits with the statement, "To know my deed 'twere best not know myself./ Wake Duncan with thy knocking. I would thou couldst." Do you think Macbeth is repenting his actions? Is there a difference between regretting an action and being repentant?

Extra Activities:

- Write a journal entry as if you were Malcolm the day after your father, the king, has been murdered. Remember that only a day or two earlier Malcolm had been named heir to the throne.

- Write (and deliver orally, if you wish) a eulogy for Duncan, remembering him as man and king. Use information from Acts I and II to discover what kind of man he was. Be creative with "examples" from his life.

- Write a poem similar to the pathetic fallacy passages, or cut out pictures from magazines to make a collage of such images.

- Discuss as a class or write a paper discussing whether prophecies, biblical and otherwise, are actually reports of what has been predetermined to happen or whether they must be consciously fulfilled.

Macbeth Study Guide

Act III

Vocabulary

A *synonym* of a word is another word with a similar meaning. Match each underlined word in the sentences below with its synonym found in the Word Box, writing the synonym in the blank provided. You may use a thesaurus.

	Word Box		
correction	honor	indestructible	holy
numerous	evil	merriment	nature
supreme	mix		

1. "Command upon me, to the which my duties are with a most <u>indissoluble</u> tie forever knit." (_____)

2. "Do you find your patience so <u>predominant</u> in your nature that you can let this go?" (_____)

3. "And thence it is that I [ask] your assistance . . ., masking the business from the common eye for <u>sundry</u> weighty reasons." (_____)

4. "Things without all <u>remedy</u> should be without regard. What's done is done." (_____)

5. "We have scorched the snake, not killed it. She'll close and be herself whilst our poor <u>malice</u> remains in danger of her former tooth." (_____)

6. "Let your remembrance apply to Banquo; present him <u>eminence</u> both with eye and tongue." (_____)

7. "Ourself will <u>mingle</u> with society and play the humble host." (_____)

8. "Here I'll sit i' th' midst. Be large in <u>mirth</u>. Anon we'll drink a measure the table round." (_____)

9. "You make me strange even to the <u>disposition</u> that I owe, when now I think you can behold such sights and keep the natural ruby of your cheeks when mine is blanched with fear." (_____)

10. "Did he not straight in <u>pious</u> rage the two delinquents tear that were the slaves of drink and thralls of sleep?" (_____)

Scrambled Quotation:

The following words are a quotation from Act III. See if you can unscramble the quotation. Next to the quotation, write the name of the person speaking and the act and scene in which it is found.

our all's is Naught's where content without desire had got spent

General Questions:

1. What is the tone of the dialogue between Macbeth and Banquo in scene i?

2. What does Macbeth decide to do about Banquo?

3. What reason does Macbeth give for not openly dealing with Banquo?

4. What is significant about Fleance's escape?

5. What does Macbeth see at the feast that no one else can see?

Analysis:

6. In Macbeth's soliloquy in scene i, lines 66–77, he says:

   > Upon my head they placed a fruitless crown . . .
   > No son of mine succeeding. If 't be so,
   > For Banquo's issue [have I done all this] . . .
   > Only for them, and mine eternal jewel
   > Given to the common enemy of man
   > To make them kings, the seeds of Banquo kings.
   > Rather than so, come fate into the list,
   > And champion me to th' utterance. . . .

What is particularly ironic about the last two lines of this quotation?

7. Referring again to the quotation in the question above, what does Macbeth mean when he says, "Only for them, and mine eternal jewel/ Given to the common enemy of man /To make them kings, the seeds of Banquo kings"?

   How does this compare to his statement in Act I, scene vii, "If th' assassination . . ./ Might be the be-all and the end-all here,/ But here, upon this bank and [shoal] of time,/ We'd jump the life to come"? Does there seem to be a change in Macbeth's attitude?

8. Although the men who come to Macbeth in Act III, scene i, are described as murderers, this seems more a stage description rather than a description of what they have done before. They appear to be merchants or farmers who have been unfairly treated and cheated out of their position. Who did they initially believe did this to them? Who does Macbeth tell them did this? What might this tell us about the kind of person Macbeth might have been prior to the start of the play?

Macbeth Study Guide

9. How does Macbeth goad the men into following his directions concerning Banquo?

10. Act III is the exact center of the play, and in it we see things begin to shift, almost as if we have crossed the center bar on a see-saw. Compare the relationship and dialogue between Macbeth and Lady Macbeth in Act III, scene ii, with that in Act I, scenes v and vii. Note how phrases and ideas once said by one character are beginning to be taken up by the other character. List two such instances.

    Lady Macbeth:

    Macbeth:

11. What might Shakespeare be foreshadowing when Macbeth wonders about Macduff's refusal to appear before him in scene iv? What, in the context of the scene, leads you to this conclusion?

12. Note how Macbeth's manhood is mentioned and/or questioned again in Act III, scene iv. Why do you think Lady Macbeth brings it up again as she did in Act I, scene vii? How does Macbeth react in this scene compared with Act I, scene vii?

13. Many scholars believe that scene v was added to the play by someone else. Compare this scene with the previous scenes with the witches. Do you think it was written by Shakespeare? Why?

14. What does scene vi tell us of the attitude toward Macbeth that is growing in Scotland? Cite examples from the text.

Dig Deeper:

15. *Parallel characters* are characters in literature that have similarities and/or face similar situations or choices. Shakespeare uses parallel characters in his plays to offer insight into the characters. In Macbeth, how are Banquo and Macbeth parallel characters? What do we learn about Macbeth's character through observing Banquo?

Macbeth Study Guide

16. When goaded by Macbeth, one of the murderers replies, "I am one, my liege,/ Whom the vile blows and buffets of the world/ Hath so incensed that I am reckless what I do/ To spite the world." Apparently he and his companion have been horribly mistreated and abused by someone. Does this justify their actions? Read Proverbs 20:22, 24:29, Romans 12:9–21. How do these verses instruct us to respond when mistreated?

17. It seems there are many people in the world who have suffered as these men have and who feel as they do. How do you feel when you have been treated unfairly? How do you want to respond? Knowing this, how should we respond to others in similar circumstances? Read Matthew 7:21 and Luke 6:27–38.

18. In scene i, Macbeth says, "To be thus is nothing,/ But to be safely thus." Later, in scene ii, Lady Macbeth says, "Naught's had, all's spent,/ Where our desire is got without content./ 'Tis safer to be that which we destroy/ Than by destruction dwell in doubtful joy."

    Paraphrase these two statements. Having gotten what they wanted, are Macbeth and Lady Macbeth happy? Why or why not? Read Proverbs 1:19 and 23:4. How do these verses fit with what Macbeth and Lady Macbeth are saying?

19. At the end of scene iv, Macbeth says, "I am in blood/ Stepped in so far that, should I wade no more,/ Returning were as tedious as go o'er." Is it ever too late to stop doing wrong? Is it ever too late to do the right thing? Why?

Discussion Questions:

- Why did Shakespeare add a third murderer in Act III, scene iii? Who might the third murder be?

- Was the ghost real or Macbeth's imagination?

Extra Activities:

- Write a dialogue between two of the lords who were present at the feast. Maybe they are meeting together later to eat the meal they didn't get to finish, or maybe they are meeting in secret. What do they think about what has gone on?

- Imagine you are Fleance, fleeing after the murder of your father. Write a journal entry, create a poem, or draw a picture expressing your feelings.

Macbeth Study Guide

Act IV

Vocabulary:

Write the letter of the definition on the right in the blank next the the word it defines.

___ 1. resolute   a. evil, corrupting, destructive

___ 2. issue   b. sound judgment

___ 3. pernicious   c. defects, failings

___ 4. exploits   d. determined, resolved, steady

___ 5. diminutive   e. small

___ 6. judicious   f. disease, sickness

___ 7. laudable   g. crave, envy

___ 8. appease   h. praiseworthy

___ 9. avarice   i. children, descendants

___ 10. coveted   j. pacify, satisfy

___ 11. malady   k. deeds, adventures

___ 12. demerits   l. greed, insatiable desire

Scrambled Quotation:

The following words are a quotation from Act I. See if you can unscramble the quotation. Next to the quotation, write the name of the person speaking and the act and scene in which it is found.

the pricking of this something comes By wicked thumbs my way

© 2000 Progeny Press

General Questions:

1. What are the witches talking about when they say, "Something wicked this way comes"? What does this tell us?

2. What three apparitions appear to Macbeth when he visits the witches again? What final vision is he given?

3. In scene i, what does Macbeth say he is willing to withstand to gain his answers?

4. What does Malcolm do to test Macduff?

Analysis:

5. Why do you think Macduff left his family when he fled to England? What do other people say about this? Do you think his wife is justified in her condemnation of him?

Macbeth Study Guide

6. Considering what has happened so far in the play, what might the Three Apparitions represent?

7. Why does Macbeth massacre Macduff's family?

8. Why does Malcolm mistrust Macduff at first?

9. The scene with the doctor in scene iii seems very strange, dropped in the midst of suspicion, fear, and descriptions of horror. What might Shakespeare be demonstrating here? How might Shakespeare be using the doctor and the descriptions of the king of England as a metaphor?

10. Contrast the king of England with Macbeth.

11. When Macduff asks Ross how his family fares under Macbeth, Ross answers, "Why, well." Why does he answer this way? What is he trying to say?

Dig Deeper:

12. How does Macduff respond to Malcolm's statement about how he would rule Scotland and what kind of man he is? What kind of behavior should we be willing to accept from our national leaders? Read Deuteronomy 17:14–20, 1 Timothy 3:1–10.

    What kind of leaders are we to be and to have as Christians? How does this apply to society at large?

13. In scene iii, Malcolm tells Duncan, "A good and virtuous nature may recoil/ In an imperial charge." In other words, "A good and honest man may feel it necessary or right to obey a ruler's unjust or reprehensible command." Read Daniel 3; 2 Samuel 24:2–4, 10–13; Romans 13:1–5; 1 Peter 2:13–17. What do these passages show or tell us about obedience to our rulers or government? How do we know whether or when to obey or disobey those in power?

Discussion Questions:

- When Macbeth is produced on stage, some productions omit Act IV, scene ii, because they believe nothing significant occurs in the action. If you were producing the play, would you include this scene? Why or why not?

Extra Activities:

- Portions of the scenes with the witches seem to have been added by a playwright other than Shakespeare at a later date. Rewrite those scenes the way you think Shakespeare might have originally written them and explain why you made the changes you did.

- Imagine you are Lady Macduff and you have just been told your husband has left the country without you, without even saying goodbye. Write a letter or a poem to him expressing your feelings.

- Imagine you are Macduff the night after learning that your family has been slaughtered by Macbeth. Though you know they will never be able to read it, write a letter or poem to your family expressing your feelings.

- Many things influence Macbeth's wrong behavior—predictions, circumstances, and people. Write a letter to Macbeth telling him how to resist temptation and peer pressure.

Act V

Vocabulary:

Define the underlined word in each sentence below using a dictionary and its context in the sentence.

1. "A great <u>perturbation</u> in nature, to receive at once the benefit of sleep and do the effects of watching."

2. "No more o' that, my lord, not more o' that. You <u>mar</u> all with this starting."

3. "Unnatural deeds do breed unnatural troubles. . . . More needs she the <u>divine</u> than the physician."

4. "Canst thou not minister to a mind diseased, . . . and with some sweet oblivious <u>antidote</u> cleanse the stuffed bosom of the perilous stuff which weighs upon the heart?"

5. "If thou couldst, doctor, . . . find her disease, and purge it to a sound and <u>pristine</u> health."

6. "What rhubarb, senna, or what <u>purgative</u> drug would scour these English hence?"

Macbeth Study Guide

7. "... none serve him but <u>constrained</u> things whose hearts are absent too."

8. "I pull in resolution and begin to doubt th' <u>equivocation</u> of the fiend, that lies like truth."

9. "Make all our trumpets speak, give them all breath, those <u>clamorous</u> harbingers of blood and death."

10. "Hail, King! for so thou art. Behold where stands th' <u>usurper's</u> cursed head. The time is free."

Scrambled Quotation:

The following words are a quotation from Act V. See if you can unscramble the quotation. Next to the quotation, write the name of the person speaking and the act and scene in which it is found.

> and then is the stage walking more struts but his poor Life's shadow heard that no player frets a hour and upon a.

General Questions:

1. What happens to Lady Macbeth in this Act?

2. What does the doctor say is wrong with Lady Macbeth? What does he suggest for her?

3. According to the lords in scene ii, how are things going for Macbeth and his rule?

4. What does Malcolm instruct his troops to do when they reach Birnam Wood? Why? Why does this affect Macbeth the way it does?

5. At the end, what does Macduff reveal that causes Macbeth to be afraid of him?

6. What happens to Macbeth's troops when Dunsinane is attacked?

Macbeth Study Guide

Analysis:

7. *Macbeth* begins and ends in battle, the first with Duncan as king, the second with Macbeth as king. Compare and contrast the two battles. Note in particular Macbeth's role and actions.

8. Looking back through the play and things Lady Macbeth has said or done, what is ironic about the following lines:

    Gentlewoman   Why, it stood by her [Lady Macbeth]. She has light by her continually. 'Tis her command.

    Lady Macbeth   Out damned spot, out, I say! . . . What, will these hands ne'er be clean? . . . Here's the smell of the blood still. All the perfumes of Arabia will not sweeten this little hand."

9. In scene i, in the famous sleepwalking scene, Lady Macbeth says,

    The Thane of Fife had a wife. Where is she now? What, will these hands ne'er be clean? No more o' that, my lord, no more o' that. You mar all with this starting.

    Consider that the Thane of Fife is Macduff, and Lady Macbeth has had no part in Macbeth's planning or murders since before the murder of Banquo. What could these lines mean for Lady Macbeth at this point?

10. What does Macbeth demand from the doctor and what does the doctor reply? What does Macbeth's response to the doctor tell us about Macbeth?

11. In scene iv, Macbeth says to the doctor, "If thou couldst, doctor, cast/ The water of my land, find her disease,/ And purge it to a sound and pristine health,/ I would applaud thee to the very echo/ That should applaud again." What is ironic about Macbeth's statement?

12. In Act III, scene iv, Macbeth says, "Strange things I have in head, that will to hand,/ Which must be acted ere they may be scanned." In other words, he has ideas that he will act upon without thinking. Look at Macbeth's behavior in Act V, scenes iii and v. How does the earlier quote explain his behavior in Act V?

Dig Deeper:

13. Note how often in Act V Macbeth reminds himself and others about his supposed invincibility and the prophecies of the witches and spirits. Why do you think this is? Read Proverbs 16:5, 18, 19. What do these verses predict for someone acting as Macbeth is?

14. When Seyton reports the death of Lady Macbeth, Macbeth responds in this way:

    > She should have died hereafter.
    > There would have been a time for such a word.
    > Tomorrow and tomorrow and tomorrow
    > Creeps in this petty pace from day to day
    > To the last syllable of recorded time,
    > And all our yesterdays have lighted fools
    > The way to dusty death. Out, out, brief candle!
    > Life's but a walking shadow, a poor player
    > That struts and frets his hour upon the stage
    > And then is heard no more. It is a tale
    > Told by an idiot, full of sound and fury,
    > Signifying nothing.
    > (scene v, lines 20–31)

    How is Macbeth affected by his wife's death? How does he seem to feel about her and about life?

15. At the end, Macbeth does not have to die—Macduff says he will not kill him if Macbeth will not fight and describes what they will do to him. Why does Macbeth not accept these conditions? Do you think Macduff describes things plainly or as a goad to Macbeth?

16. Assuming proper trial and guilt, do you think a person like the person Macbeth has become should be allowed to live if he is captured or surrenders?

17. Toward the end of scene viii, Siward learns of his son's death. How does he respond to this news? Why do you think he responds this way?

Extra Activities:

- Draw or paint a picture of Lady Macbeth sleepwalking.

- If Lady Macbeth had left a suicide note, what do you think it would have said?

- Imagine you are Lady Macbeth's gentlewoman. Write a letter to your sister describing all that has happened.

Macbeth Study Guide

Overview

1. Do you think Macbeth or Lady Macbeth ever felt guilty for or repented of what they did, or do you think they regretted only that their actions were not successful? Give examples from the play for each of them to support your answer.

2. An *extended metaphor* is a metaphor that is repeated within a portion of a work or throughout the entire work. For example, in *Macbeth* Shakespeare repeatedly uses robes or clothing as metaphors for honor and station. Find instances of this metaphor in the play and explain why it is particularly appropriate in *Macbeth*.

3. Within the context of this play, do you think Macbeth is redeemable? If not, explain why not. If so, do you think there comes a point at which he is beyond hope? Describe that point and why you think it is significant.

Macbeth Study Guide

4. Much of the action and drama of Macbeth deals with how he responds to prophecies he receives. Look up these biblical responses to prophecy or commandment:

   Abraham—Genesis 15:4–6, 16:1–12, 17:15–21

   Jacob—Genesis 25:21–26, 27:1–45

   Gideon—Judges 6:11–7:25

   David—1 Samuel 16:1–13, 18:1–10, 24:1–22, 26:1–11, 31:1–7, 2 Samuel 2:1–4.

   How are the passages about Abraham and Jacob similar to each other? How are the passages about Gideon and David different? What general rule can we glean from these examples?

5. Compare the fates of Macbeth and Lady Macbeth. Which one do you think is most tragic? Do you believe either one understood the enormity of their actions or the consequences of their actions?

6. Macbeth is a play filled with death. How do the characters within the play respond to the deaths of those close to them? Give examples from the play. Why do you think these people respond as they do?

Macbeth Study Guide

7. In the beginning of the play, Lady Macbeth seems in control and confident, but by the end of the play she seems weak and insignificant, certainly mad. At what point do things start to change for her? Use examples from the play to support your answer.

8. How does Macbeth change throughout the play? What effect does becoming king seem to have on him?

9. Read Luke 9:23–25. How do these verses apply to Macbeth? What do these verses mean to you and your life?

10. The main character in a work of fiction is called the *protagonist* and is often the hero of the work, though some protagonists are evil. In most works the protagonist grows or changes after the climax of the story. A *tragic hero* is a protagonist who brings about his own downfall by a choice brought on or influenced by a character flaw, and traditionally by the end of the story he recognizes that he has brought about his own downfall. An *antihero* is a protagonist who simply lacks heroic qualities, who is the opposite of what we expect a hero to be.

    Based on what you have read, what kind of protagonist is Macbeth? (Feel free to look these terms up in a good literary terms dictionary for more complete definitions.) Does he differ in some ways from the classic definition? Use examples from the play to illustrate your answer.

Macbeth Study Guide

11. In Act V, scene iii, Macbeth says,

    > I have lived long enough. My way of life
    > Is fall'n into the sere, the yellow leaf,
    > And that which should accompany old age,
    > As honor, love, obedience, troops of friends,
    > I must not look to have, but in their stead
    > Curses, not loud but deep, mouth-honor, breath
    > Which the poor heart would fain deny and dare not.

    In Act V, scene v, he says,

    > Tomorrow and tomorrow and tomorrow
    > Creeps in this petty pace from day to day
    > To the last syllable of recorded time,
    > And all our yesterdays have lighted fools
    > The way to dusty death. Out, out, brief candle!
    > Life's but a walking shadow, a poor player
    > That struts and frets his hour upon the stage
    > And then is heard no more. It is a tale
    > Told by an idiot, full of sound and fury,
    > Signifying nothing.

    Read Ecclesiastes 1 and 2. How do these verses compare with Macbeth's statements? Read Ephesians 2:1–10. Where do these verses say our hope is?

12. In Act I, scene vii, Macbeth says,

    > If th' assassination
    > Could trammel up the consequence and catch
    > With his surcease success, that but this blow
    > Might be the be-all and the end-all here,

Macbeth Study Guide

> But here, upon this bank and shoal of time,
> We'd jump the life to come. But in these cases
> We still have judgment here. . . .

What is Macbeth saying is most important to him? Is it common for people to think this way about their actions? Read 2 Corinthians 5:6–10, Philippians 1:20–26, 3:7–11. In these verses, what does Paul say is most important to him? Which goal would last the longest and have the biggest benefit?

13. Foreshadowing is, in a sense, an author's prophecy for future events in a story; and often, like prophecy, the message is not fully clear until much later. After the following quotations, write the events the statements foreshadowed. You should look the quotations up to see the context in which they were made.

    > *Banquo*   But 'tis strange.
    > And oftentimes, to win us to our harm,
    > The instruments of darkness tell us truths,
    > Win us with honest trifles, to betray 's
    > In deepest consequence.
    > (Act I, scene iii)

    > *Duncan*   There's no art
    > To find the mind's construction in the face.
    > He was a gentleman on whom I built
    > An absolute trust.
    > (Act I, scene iv)

> *Macbeth*   Had I but died an hour before this chance,
> I had lived a blessed time; for from this instant
> There's nothing serious in mortality.
> All is but toys. Renown and grace is dead.
> The wine of life is drawn, and the mere lees
> Is left this vault to brag of.
> (Act II, scene iii)

14. Although it is clear that the prophecies handed down in *Macbeth* were not from God (after all, they were given by witches), sometimes more "agreeable" people proclaim they have messages from God. How are we to know whom to believe? Read Deuteronomy 13:1–3, 18:21–22; Matthew 7:15–20; and 1 John 4:1–6.

15. By the end of the play—in fact, by Act III—Macbeth believes his soul to be lost and condemned for his murders. This seems to be one of the reasons he wades so deeply in the violence he commits. Read John 5:24, John 3:16–18, 1 John 4:9–10, Romans 3:10–24, Ephesians 2:1–14, Colossians 2:13–15. Are we without hope before God because of past sins? Can anyone earn God's favor and salvation? What brings us to God and salvation?

Writing Projects

1. Look through the play at the times fate is mentioned and how it is treated by the characters. Write a paper dealing with these questions: 1) What is fate? 2) Are the statements by the witches and the Apparitions fate? 3) How does Macbeth deal with the idea of fate? Is he consistent? 4) How does Banquo deal with the idea of fate? 5) Is fate a biblical idea? Cite scripture to support your position.

2. Write a paper summarizing the basic concepts of the following philosophies: pragmatism, humanism, materialism, nihilism. Which philosophy most closely fits Macbeth? Which one most closely describes you? Read Psalms 119, Mark 12:28–34, Romans 12. On what are Christians to base their life and actions?

3. Write a short paper comparing heraldry (the English form of family succession) to tanistry (the Scottish form of succession). Explain the merits and problems with each and how the two systems are reflected in *Macbeth*.

4. A lot of debate has gone into how Shakespeare portrays women in *Macbeth*. Are they strong? Are they all, in a sense "witches" or helpless? Write a paper exploring the role of women in *Macbeth*. You may wish to look up some of the commentaries and compare your ideas to what others have said.

5. A number of potential themes run through *Macbeth*: misuse of power, light versus darkness, natural versus the unnatural, good versus evil, insanity, fate, ambition, guilt, and more. Pick a theme that you see running through *Macbeth* and write a paper exploring how the play deals with that theme. Tie it in with scriptures that also deal with the theme, and explain whether you feel the play leads to the same conclusion the scriptures do.

Macbeth Study Guide

6. Read the Greek tragedy *Oedipus the King*. Write an essay discussing similarities and differences between Oedipus and Macbeth.

7. Write a paper, or hold a class debate, on whether a person's life is predetermined by fate (or by God) or whether people have free will to act. Research your position by looking through the Bible and writings by philosophers and theologians for topics such as self-determination, predestination, foreknowledge, free will, etc.

8. Is there a hero in *Macbeth?* Discuss your reasons for your answer, using quotations from the play to support your reasoning.

Macbeth Study Guide

Answer Key

Act I
Vocabulary:
1. d; 2. h; 3. i; 4. b; 5. j; 6. a; 7. e; 8. f; 9. g; 10. c
Scrambled Quotation:
There's no art to find the mind's construction in the face.—Duncan, Act I, scene iv.
General Questions:
1. Macbeth and, apparently to a lesser degree, Banquo.
2. Three witches meet Macbeth and Banquo on the heath and tell Macbeth that he will gain the title Thane of Cawdor and reign as king. They tell Banquo that though he will never be king, his descendants will.
3. Macbeth is referring to Duncan's son Malcolm. Macbeth means that Malcolm must be removed for Macbeth to gain Duncan's throne.
4. Macbeth and his wife have decided to kill Duncan by getting his attendants drunk, murdering him in his sleep, then blaming the murder on the drunken attendants.
Analysis:
5. Answers will vary, but there is a sense of foreboding and chaos in this first scene that will carry throughout the play, particularly as it reflects Macbeth. There is also a staccato tempo to the scene and language that seems nonsensical, laying the groundwork for the rapid scene changes and rush of events to come.
6. This is ironic because we know Macbeth is considering treason. Macbeth, like his predecessor, is a man Duncan trusts but who will betray Duncan in the end.
7. Answers may vary. The clearest example is Lady Macbeth, who in scene v calls upon the spirits to "unsex me here," "make thick my blood," "take my milk for gall." Again, in scene vii, she describes a willingness to pluck her nursing child from her breast and dash his brains out. Her words draw an immediate comparison to the Weird Sisters, who "should be women" but apparently are not. She renounces her womanhood and her motherhood. In fact, she seems to be willing to give up her humanity. This is unnatural and, we can safely say, bad.
8. Answers and examples will vary. Following are some of the character traits students should find and give examples for:
<u>Macbeth</u>—brave and valiant in battle, loyal in the past, a leader, ambitious, possibly morally ambivalent, malleable, possibly insecure about his manliness.
<u>Lady Macbeth</u>—ambitious, cruel, manipulative, devious, amoral.
<u>Duncan</u>—kind, trusting, perhaps not a good judge of character, generous
<u>Banquo</u>—brave and valiant in battle, loyal, forthright, a leader, ambitious, moral or at least ethical.
9. In Act I, Macbeth is the only character to speak in asides, although Banquo answers some of Macbeth's asides. Macbeth has seven asides in scene iii; Banquo answers two asides. Suddenly, in scene iii, Macbeth and Banquo have secrets—the witches' prophecies. The number of asides Macbeth makes seems to indicate a strong inner struggle with his forgotten or suppressed ambition to be king and his sudden murderous thoughts. Many of the asides seem to be made almost as if Macbeth's thoughts and struggle have made him forget other characters are even present (Banquo: "Look how our partner's rapt"). It appears Macbeth suddenly harbors internal turmoil and secrets.
10. The witches statement reflects how things are rapidly being turned on their head—there has been treachery by Cawdor, battle from which good has come, and now a prophecy for Macbeth that appears set to disrupt everything. Note that Macbeth and his wife deliberately choose to appear fair but be foul: "look like the innocent flower, but be the serpent under it," Act I, scene v; "False face must hide what the false heart doth know," Act I, scene vii. Faith, trust, and loyalty are about to be cast aside and to be not as they appear.
11. Answers will vary, but his quickly shifting fortunes seems to have Macbeth badly off balance. He comes from a bitterly fought and bloody battle to an empty heath to be confronted by three witch-apparitions who prophecy his gaining the title Thane of Cawdor and king. Before he can assimilate this or decide whether he believes it, Ross conveys to him the new title of thane, and the prophecy appears fate. Then he meets Duncan, who seems to dash the prophecy by naming his son Malcolm as heir-apparent. Macbeth then rushes home, where his wife greets him and pushes him to finalize or fulfill the prophecy himself. Act I feels as if it has taken place within a period of hours, although the true action would have taken a day or so. Macbeth has had little time to reflect on events and their meanings.

© 2000 Progeny Press

Macbeth Study Guide

12. Lady Macbeth says Macbeth is "too full o' th' milk of human kindness," that he has ambition but wants to accomplish his goals in a holy (or at least ethical) manner and does not want to be false to those in authority. Answers may vary. By "illness" Lady Macbeth refers to a ruthlessness that she sees as necessary to accomplishing one's goals. Macbeth, she says, has ambition but lacks ruthlessness. She vows to force him to overcome his scruples.

13. Macbeth begins thinking of murder almost as soon as he is told he is Thane of Cawdor and begins believing he may become king. In an aside toward the end of Act I, scene iii, Macbeth says, "why do I yield to that suggestion/ Whose horrid image doth unfix my hair/ And make my seated heart knock at my ribs/ . . . My thought, whose murder yet is but fantastical,/ Shakes so my single state of mind/ That function is smothered in surmise. . . ." Answers will vary about what this tells us about Macbeth. It seems that though he appears very upright and honorable on the surface, inside he may be an opportunist, selfish, and ambitious, and to believe that the ends justify the means. It is difficult to tell whether he is struggling with whether to do right or wrong, or whether he is shocked at the corruption already present.

14. Answers will vary, but should be along these lines: Duncan and Banquo describe the castle as pleasant, like a temple. Banquo says "heaven's breath/ Smells wooingly here"; he implies the castle is blessed. Unlike its pleasant exterior, however, Macbeth and his wife are plotting murder, using terms of gross imagery, including infanticide. Duncan speaks of the love he receives and the beneficence and love he gives. His attitude is one of great friendship and ease. In this encounter, Lady Macbeth speaks only of honor and duty, nothing of love; but in the surrounding scenes we see the gross and horrific language she uses planning Duncan's murder. As we seen in much of Act I, outward appearances are often opposite of the inward reality.

Dig Deeper:

15. Abishai is convinced that this is the fulfillment of the prophecy, that God has delivered Saul into David's hands so that he can kill him and become king. David refuses to take the fulfillment of the prophecy into his own hands and offend God by killing his anointed king. David also refuses to allow Abishai to kill Saul. In essence, David tells Abishai that God did anoint David king, but he has not yet removed the previous king whom he also anointed. Until God does so, no one has the right to remove the current anointed king. Macbeth and his wife clearly see things the same way Abishai does. To them, the presence of Duncan in their home implies that he has been delivered into their hands and they should take advantage of this. Note that Macbeth is less certain of this than his wife is.

16. Macbeth talks about the prophecy and his inner thoughts only with his wife. Because she is his wife, her perspective might well be similar to his—he ended up with little or no real discussion of the rightness, or even the feasibility, of their plans. These verses all promote seeking advisers and advice for our actions, particularly if they are momentous. Advisers often see things one does not and are not as affected by the emotions of personal involvement. Godly advisers often can direct our eyes back to what is concrete and scriptural.

17. Lady Macbeth seems to equate action with manliness—"Art thou afeard/ To be the same in thine own act and valor/ As thou art in desire?" "When you durst do it, then you were a man;/ And to be more than what you were, you would/ Be so much more the man" (in other words, when you were willing to murder Duncan, then you were a man; and to actually murder him and become king would make you even more of a man). She does not discuss the rightness or wisdom of their plans, she just berates Macbeth for failing to follow through, for appearing a coward. In contrast, the chapters in Proverbs direct a man to wisdom and understanding. Only by embracing wisdom—wisdom "from the knowledge of God"—can a man know when and how to act. This is what marks a true man—wisdom, justice, and honor.

18. Answers will vary. Macbeth says that if the murder and all its consequences could be wrapped up in one event and he could get it all over with, he would, without any thought to what might come in the afterlife. But such events have consequences here on earth, too. He fears that whatever he does will come back upon himself. He recognizes his duties as relative, subject, and host, and acknowledges that Duncan has been a good and humble king. All this makes him realize that others will likely condemn and be horrified by his deed, and the only reason he has for acting is for his own ambition. Macbeth does not seem to have any true sense of right and wrong. He is not concerned with God or eternity, only with what will get him what he wants on earth. He is concerned with how people will react to his actions only because he may get punished for them. There is no real consideration of what he or Duncan deserve, just what Macbeth can get away with. Macbeth has no scruples, considering only what is to his advantage.

19. These verses encourage the readers to concentrate on their walk with Christ and to not let anyone distract them or turn them aside. Though Macbeth does not seem to have had a relationship with God, he appears to have at least been honorable and loyal, or acted that way, and it is these things that have won him the position and acclaim that he now enjoys. It seems odd that, having gained them through honesty, he now seems ready to discard all of that and become

treacherous. Answers may vary. Somehow people often seem willing to try the method that seems fastest and easiest, and sin often promises a fast, easy way to reach our goals. We can guard against this by reading God's word regularly, praying, and seeking advice from godly people we trust.

Act II
Vocabulary:
1. a; 2. c; 3. c; 4. a; 5. b; 6. c; 7. b; 8. a
Scrambled Quotation:
Merciful powers, restrain in me the cursed thoughts that nature gives way to in repose.—Banquo, Act II, scene i
General Questions:
1. Banquo and Fleance, his son, decide it is after midnight. The late and lonely hour, what some call the "witching hour," fit the murderous actions of Macbeth and his wife.
2. A dagger, first clean, then bloody, seems to hover before Macbeth.
3. The porter in scene iii.
4. The porter imagines himself to be porter to the gates of hell. He admits he has been drinking heavily, so it is unclear whether he is imagining he truly is in hell or whether he is just being fanciful. His imaginings are particularly apt, however, considering what is happening in the castle.
5. Macbeth kills Duncan during the night and his two groomsmen the next morning, claiming he is overcome with anger and outrage at Duncan's murder.
6. Malcolm and Donalbain decide that whoever killed their father may be planning to kill them also, so they flee—Malcolm to England and Donalbain to Ireland. People immediately begin to suspect that they hired Duncan's groomsmen to kill him.
Analysis:
7. When one of the sleepers says "God bless us," Macbeth cannot say "Amen." It actually may seem a little absurd that Macbeth feels he should say "amen" to the man's "God bless us." Macbeth has just murdered his cousin and king as he lay sleeping. His hands are bloody and his conscience is black. Though he knows he needs God's blessing, he cannot ask for it because, though he may be horrified at his actions, he apparently is unrepentant.
8. Answers will vary. We see Banquo with his son, Fleance, having a normal father/son chat, compared with the brutal discussions Macbeth has had with his wife. Note also that Macbeth seems to have no offspring. (A small historical note: The true Lady Macbeth was apparently widowed before she married Macbeth, which explains how she can know motherhood, yet Macbeth has no heir.) Banquo is trying to avoid, and asks for divine help in conquering, the disturbing thoughts the witches' prophecy has raised in him ("Merciful powers,/ Restrain in me the cursèd thoughts that nature/ Gives way to in repose."). Also, when Macbeth hints that Banquo would gain benefit by taking Macbeth's counsel, Banquo responds that he will be happy to consider Macbeth's counsel so long as he can do so honorably, remain true to himself, and have no strings attached. Macbeth has not been fighting very hard against the ambition the prophecy aroused within him. Though he has qualms, they are only about punishment and the trouble that might fall upon him. He is not concerned about right, honor, or justice.
9. Answers will vary. A paraphrase should be something along the following lines: Macbeth: "If you'll follow my lead (OR If you'll join me) (OR If you'll go along with my counsel), I'll make sure you are rewarded (OR I'll make sure you receive honor)." Banquo: "If I lose no honor in trying to gain more, but keep true to what I believe in (OR keep my spirit free) and am not obligated to you, then I will listen." Macbeth is trying to sound Banquo out on whether Banquo will follow him, trying to get a commitment from Banquo without actually revealing his plans. Banquo's answer is trouble because it reveals that Banquo will follow his ideals, not the easiest or most profitable path, and Macbeth clearly has no use for ideals. Macbeth will be able to rely on Banquo's support only if Banquo believes the cause is just.
10. There are many examples possible; we will list a number, but not all.
<u>Personification:</u>
"Thou sure and firm-set earth, Hear not my steps";
"The bell invites me";
"Some say the earth was feverish and did shake";
"Confusion now hath made his masterpiece. . . .";
"dark night strangles the traveling lamp";

"living light should kiss it."

<u>Pathetic fallacy</u>:

Ross: Ha, good father,/ Thou seest the heavens, as troubled with man's act,/ Threatens his bloody stage. By th' clock 'tis day,/ And yet dark night strangles the traveling lamp./ Is 't night's predominance or the day's shame/ That darkness does the face of earth entomb/ When living light should kiss it?

Old Man: 'Tis unnatural,/ Even like the deed that's done. On Tuesday last/ A falcon, tow'ring in her pride of place,/ Was by a mousing owl hawked at and killed.

Ross And Duncan's horses . . . Turned wild in nature, broke their stalls, flung out,/ Contending 'gainst obedience, as they would/ Make war with mankind.

Old Man: 'Tis said they eat each other.

11. Macbeth begins to see and hear things ("Is this a dagger which I see before me," Act II, scene i; "Who's there? what, ho!" Act II, scene ii; "Didst thou not hear a noise?" same scene; "Methought I heard a voice cry 'Sleep no more!'" same scene). Answers will vary, but Macbeth seems to realize the immensity of his deeds without being willing to stop himself. He may believe they will ultimately fail, or he may see the fullness of his crime against God and nature. He seems frightened.

12. Shakespeare is known for his fluid and lyrical dialogue, but in this instance it is almost staccato, particularly in the following exchange:

Lady Macbeth: Did you not speak?

Macbeth: When?

Lady Macbeth: Now.

Macbeth: As I descended?

Lady Macbeth: Ay.

Macbeth: Hark!—Who lies i' th' second chamber?

Lady Macbeth: Donalbain.

The tempo is feverish, as is Macbeth.

13. Answers will vary. <u>Understatement</u>: 1) "Macduff: Is the King stirring, worthy thane? Macbeth: Not yet." This would be ironic because we know the king to be dead and he will never stir again. 2) "Lennox: The night has been unruly. Where we lay,/ Our chimneys were blown down and, as they say,/ Lamentings heard i' th' air, strange screams of death,/ And prophesying, with accents terrible,/ Of dire combustion and confused events/ New hatched to th' woeful time. The obscure bird/ Clamored the livelong night. Some say the earth/ Was feverous and did shake. Macbeth: 'Twas a rough night." This is ironic also, both because Macbeth's response seems inadequate to Lennox's description and because of Macbeth's act of murder. <u>Hyperbole</u>: The entire scene with the porter could be considered hyperbole to humorous effect. Most of what Macduff and Macbeth say after the discovery of Duncan's body is hyperbole, but in this case it is for dramatic effect. Some of Macbeth's statements can be considered ironic because we know it was he who killed the king.

14. Macbeth probably was too distracted by what was about to happen when they discover Duncan's body to talk much with Lennox. After Duncan's body is found, Macbeth seems to go to great lengths to prove his "love" to Duncan, both in killing the groomsmen and in long, picturesque speech. Lady Macbeth appears to faint either to add her own drama to the scene or to stop her husband's wild, almost outlandish, claims of love and loyalty for Duncan. Their actions after the discovery of Duncan's body are also similar to what they say they will do at the end of Act I.

15. The word repeated is *sleep*. After Macbeth has murdered Duncan and returned to his wife, he tells her, "Methought I heard a voice cry 'Sleep no more!/ Macbeth does murder sleep'—the innocent sleep,/ Sleep that knits up the raveled sleave of care. . . ." The repetition of sleep continues for several lines more. Answers may vary about the significance or meaning of the repetition. Most likely, judging from what Macbeth says within these lines, sleep is a metaphor for peace—both peace of mind and peace in general.

16. Answers will vary. He reports what people are saying and does not contradict it, yet there is a sense that he does not wholly believe it. Note that he refuses to go to Scone to attend Macbeth's coronation.

Dig Deeper:

17. Duncan's sons realize that they do not yet feel the great loss that those around them are professing and fear that their apparent lack of grief will bring suspicion on them. They also fear that whoever killed their father will try to kill them next. Answers will vary.

18. Only God can cleanse us of sin. He desires repentance and an honest turning to him.

Macbeth Study Guide

19. The three things described by Lennox and the old man are the unnatural darkness of the day ("dark night strangles the traveling lamp"); a mousing owl that kills a falcon; and Duncan's horses that fight against obedience, "make war with mankind," and "eat each other." Answers will vary. In each case, a "lesser" thing has risen over a "greater" thing. For example darkness has conquered the sun, a small owl has killed a great falcon, and well-trained horses now fight against people. These could all be metaphors for the lesser Macbeth killing King Duncan. The horses eating each other could also refer to the later events of Macbeth killing fellow thanes and the general distrust that grows between the thanes of Scotland.

20. Answers will vary. Regret can occur for a number of reasons: believing an action is wrong, finding events do not turn out as planned, wishing circumstances were different. Repentance recognizes that something was wrong and that correction has to take place. The original meaning of the word was to turn around and go the other direction.

Act III
Vocabulary:
1. indestructible; 2. supreme; 3. numerous; 4. correction; 5. evil; 6. honor; 7. mix; 8. merriment; 9. nature; 10. holy

Scrambled Quotation:
Naught's had, all's spent, where our desire is got without content.—Lady Macbeth, Act III, scene ii.

General Questions:
1. Answers will vary. It appears that the two will be polite to each other, but neither trusts the other anymore. Note that Macbeth keeps asking one more question about what Banquo will be doing that day and Banquo is careful to answer without any detail.
2. Macbeth hires some desperate peasants to kill Banquo and Fleance.
3. He tells the peasant men that he could not openly deal with Banquo himself because it would destroy the loyalty of mutual friends and subjects. If his cause was just, this would not be so.
4. Fleance's escape is significant because Fleance is alive to fulfill the witches' prophecy to Banquo.
5. Macbeth sees the dead Banquo sitting in his chair.

Analysis:
6. Macbeth murdered Duncan and gained the crown because of the prophecy of the three witches. Now, however, he is angry that all that he "sacrificed" for will be given over to Banquo's descendants—again, as prophesied by the witches'—and he determines to challenge and fight "fate" to the death. He is willing to "accept" fate when it is in his favor, but he challenges fate when it seems against him.
7. The quotation from Act III could be paraphrased: "Only for Banquo's sons have I sold my eternal soul to the devil." The quotation from Act I could be paraphrased: "If there could be no consequences to the assassination in this life, I wouldn't care about my soul in the next life." Macbeth seems be more concerned about his legacy than he was in Act I, and he seems to regret "selling" his soul, committing such great evil, for the temporary crown of king. He now wishes that he could at least pass it on to his descendants. He seems to be valuing his soul more highly, but already counting it as lost.
8. The men initially believed that Macbeth was the cause of their loss and degradation, but Macbeth convinces them Banquo was at fault. The men's earlier conviction that Macbeth was behind their downfall, if correct (and Macbeth certainly has reason to lie about Banquo), could mean that Macbeth was not the pinnacle of virtue he seemed before the witches' prophecy. It implies that he was always willing to take what he could when he was able to get away with it. For an example of this type of behavior, see 1 Kings 21:1–15.
9. First he tells them that Banquo was the cause of all their hardships. Then he taunts them about their patience, "Do you find/ Your patience so predominant in your nature/ That you can let this go? Are you so gospeled/ To pray for this good man and for his issue,/ Whose heavy hand hath bowed you to the grave/ And beggared you forever?" In essence, Macbeth calls them "goody-two-shoes" and questions their willingness to act. When they respond, "We are men, my liege," Macbeth challenges their manhood: "Ay, in the catalogue you go for men,/ As hounds and greyhounds, mongrels, spaniels, curs,/ Shoughs, water-rugs, and demi-wolves are clept/ All by the name of dogs. . . . And so of men./ Now, if you have a station in the file,/ Not i' th' worst of rank of manhood, say 't,/ And I will put that business in your bosoms." In other words, "You are men like all breeds of dog are dog, but if you're not of the weakest, lowest form of man say so and I'll give you this job to do." This seems to be the same sort of argument that Lady Macbeth used on him, and it works on these peasants also.

© 2000 Progeny Press

Macbeth Study Guide

10. Answers may vary. 1) Lady Macbeth: devises the plan to kill Duncan (Act I, scene vii); Macbeth: devises the plan to kill Banquo and Fleance (Act III, scene i). 2) Macbeth wanted to enjoy his new-found favor with the king, "He hath honored me of late, and I have bought/ Golden opinions from all sorts of people,/ Which would be worn now in their newest gloss" (Act I, scene vii); Lady Macbeth wishes to enjoy, as far as possible, their new position, "Things without all remedy should be without regard," "Be bright and jovial/ Among your guests tonight" (Act III scene ii). 3) Lady Macbeth says she will take care of things and tells Macbeth not to worry: "you shall put/ This night's great business into my dispatch... Leave all the rest to me" (Act I, scene v); Macbeth says he is taking care of things and she need not worry: "Be innocent of the knowledge, dearest chuck,/ Till thou applaud the deed" (Act III, scene ii). 4) Lady Macbeth: "Look like th' innocent flower,/ But be the serpent under 't" (Act I, scene v); Macbeth: "And make our faces vizards to our hearts,/ Disguising what they are" (Act III, scene ii).

11. Answers will vary. It seems to bode ill for Macduff that Macbeth's attention suddenly focuses on him at this point. Macbeth seems distracted and disturbed in his thoughts; they jump from blood and fantastic scenes to wondering about the time, then turn to Macduff. He also mentions that he has spies in everyone's house, and that he is in blood so deep he might as well continue.

12. Answers will vary. Almost as soon as Macbeth sees the ghost and begins acting strangely, Lady Macbeth pulls him aside and demands, "Are you a man?" and then she repeats it again shortly, "What, quite unmanned in folly?" She seems to use this challenge when keeping Macbeth in line or chastising him. Macbeth does not act cowed, however, as he did in Act I, instead answering, "Ay, and a bold one, that dare look on that/ Which might appall the devil." Perhaps because of what they have been through, perhaps because he knows he is facing an enemy and he is a warrior, he does not back down or equivocate. He seems little affected by Lady Macbeth's taunt. Perhaps her taunt sounds paltry next to what Macbeth has done and next to the image of the ghost. To the ghost, Macbeth challenges, "What man dare, I dare," echoing his statement to Lady Macbeth in Act I, scene vii, "I dare do all that may become a man. Who dares [do] more is none." He admits that he trembles before the ghost, but he also now seems to know what he is capable of.

13. Answers will vary. The scene does little for the play, adds no real information, and does not further the plot. The rhythm of the lines differs from most dialogue in Macbeth, and the entire scene is written in rhyme, the extent of which was unusual for Shakespeare.

14. Answers may vary. Though Lennox and the unnamed lord are not open or direct about their doubts and disdain for Macbeth, it is clear from their statements that they no longer believe that Malcolm, Donalbain, or Fleance killed their fathers or that they would live long if Macbeth found them. There are a number of examples. Lennox is sarcastic in a number of his statements, "Banquo walked too late,/ Whom you may say, if 't please you, Fleance killed,/ For Fleance fled. Men must not walk too late." The other lord makes clear people long for things as they had been before Macbeth, "That, by the help of these (with Him above/ To ratify the work), we may again/ Give to our tables meat, sleep to our nights/ Free from our feasts and banquets bloody knives,/ Do faithful homage, and receive free honors,/ All which we pine for now."

Dig Deeper:

15. Banquo and Macbeth are parallel characters because they hold similar positions in the kingdom, are the heroes of the opening battles, are both given prophecies, and both have to choose how to respond to the prophecies. By observing Banquo's struggle against and rejection of evil, we see more clearly Macbeth's unwillingness to restrain his ambition and his decent into evil.

16. These verses warn us about seeking revenge on our own terms and tell us to leave revenge to God. Instead we are to repay hate with love, persecution with blessing. We are to love and nurture each other and live at peace with everyone, as far as we are able.

17. Answers will vary. Though it is not right to react to injustice with anger, we should understand when other people do. We will be judged as we judge and treat other people. We cannot erase past injustice, but we can show them the love God has for us and for them, and we should treat them as compassionately as we would want to be treated.

18. Answers will vary. Macbeth is saying, "Everything I have is worthless unless I know I can't lose it." Lady Macbeth is saying, "We don't have anything yet because none of it is solid or secure. It's safer to be a victim than to be a destroyer who can't hold onto what she gets." Macbeth and his wife are not happy because they are afraid of losing everything. The verses from Proverbs reinforce what they are saying—ill-gotten gain consumes you and can disappear quickly.

19. Answers will vary.

Macbeth Study Guide

Act IV
Vocabulary:
1. d; 2. i; 3. a; 4. k; 5. e; 6. b; 7. h; 8. j; 9. l; 10. g; 11. f; 12. c

Scrambled Quotation:
By the pricking of my thumbs, something wicked this way comes.—Second Witch, Act IV, scene i.

General Questions:
1. The witches are talking about Macbeth. This tells us that they now consider Macbeth wicked.
2. The first three apparitions are an Armed Head, a Bloody Child, and a Child Crowned. When Macbeth demands to know whether Banquo's descendants will reign, he sees a group of eight kings and Banquo.
3. Macbeth says though the witches call down a hellish storm that would destroy all that is natural and holy, "Even till destruction sicken" itself, he demands answers to his questions. Note that Macbeth no longer cares anything for consequences, particularly consequences for others, as long as he gets what he wants.
4. Malcolm claims to be even more degenerate than Macbeth, first claiming overwhelming lust and avarice, then declaring that if he gained power there is no evil he would not do: "I should/ Pour the sweet milk of concord into hell,/ Uproar the universal peace, confound/ All unity on earth."

Analysis:
5. Answers will vary. Macduff never gives a reason for his actions; he may have felt he had to act with as much speed as possible. He may have assumed Macbeth would act with chivalry toward women and children. Others question his motives, however; Malcolm questions why he would do such a thing, certainly Macduff's wife does. Macbeth's murder of Macduff's family seems to make her fears justified, but probably everyone assumed the greatest threat was that Macbeth would hold them hostage.
6. Answers will vary. Considering the events so far and what has been prophesied, the Armed Head is likely to represent Duncan and his murder by Macbeth; the Bloody Child likely represents Banquo and his murder by Macbeth in an attempt to frustrate the prophecy that Banquo's descendants would reign as kings, or it could represent Macduff's murdered children; and the Crowned Child likely represents the frustration of Macbeth's designs and the ascension to the crown of Banquo's heirs. Oddly, Macbeth sees no significance in the forms of the apparitions, and, perhaps frighteningly, the gory image of a bloody child does not even draw comment from Macbeth.
7. Answers will vary. Actually, there appears to be little reason beyond the fact that Macbeth was angry with Macduff. He says "From this moment/ The very firstlings of my heart shall be/ The firstlings of my hand," in other words, "I'll do whatever I think of without pausing to consider." He couldn't kill Macduff, so he took out his fury on everyone in his household. We're beginning to see Macbeth lose perspective, to see him act without restraint and out of all proportion.
8. Malcolm points out that Macduff has not been harmed by Macbeth, though Macduff claims Macbeth is devouring Scotland. He also points out that Macduff may honestly believe it his duty to deliver Malcolm to Scotland's present king, and that Macduff has left his family behind, which implies either that Macduff has nothing to fear from Macbeth or that they may already be in Macbeth's control and are being used to control Macduff. Malcolm later adds that Macbeth has already tried to get to him using similar means.
9. Just before the doctor appears in this scene, Macduff has been describing the horrors that have been occurring in Scotland, and between Malcolm and Macduff we have seen the distrust these events have bred. Soon, Ross enters and tells of the fighting and rebellions in Scotland and of the murder of Macduff's family. But right in the middle we have a description of the sanctity and powers of the king of England. Shakespeare seems to be doing several things: 1) demonstrating that the world has not succumbed to evil, only Macbeth has; 2) that outside Scotland the power of heaven still reigns, 3) that the healing power of virtue is about to do battle with the disease of Scotland. In the middle of descriptions of horror, distrust, murder, and rebellion, we have a description of the healing powers of the king of England, "at his touch/ (Such sanctity hath heaven given his hand)/ They presently amend." Malcolm describes it, "How he solicits heaven/ Himself best knows, but strangely visited people/ All swoll'n and ulcerous, pitiful to the eye,/ The mere despair of surgery, he cures." The literal healing power of the king here is used as a metaphor for the healing he can give Scotland; as he cures the "swoll'n and ulcerous" people, so will he heal the open wound of Scotland by sending troops and supporting Malcolm. Note that after the appearance of the doctor and the revelation of the murders of Macduff's family, Macduff and Malcolm agree to move against Macbeth in force and with the help of England—a change for the better and one that can safely be assumed to eventually lead to the cleansing of Scotland.

© 2000 Progeny Press

10. Several contrasts can be observed here: The king of England is a healer—Macbeth is a warrior and now a murderer. The king of England gets his power from God—Macbeth goes to the witches. The king has "a heavenly gift of prophecy"—Macbeth has no such gift, but relies on the prophecies of the witches.

11. Ross seems to be trying to tell Macduff of the murders of his family, but appears unable to actually say the words. To our ears it sounds as if he is being insensitive and toying with words, but his words or manner clearly convey something of the meaning because Macduff presses him and finally insists "Be not a niggard of your speech. How goes 't?" (Note that *niggard* means "a meanly covetous and stingy person," a miser.) His statements that they are "well" and "at peace" may be compared to someone starting bad news by saying, "They didn't suffer" or "At least they are in a better place."

Dig Deeper:

12. Macduff's first responses to Malcolm's description of his character are disturbing; he tries to justify Malcolm's defects and, if not accept them, at least overlook them. He declares that though lust has dethroned many kings, there are enough "willing" women that it need not be a problem to others, and though avarice was "worse," there are plenty of lands and riches in Scotland for the king so that he need not take much of others. Finally, however, Malcolm's list of flaws becomes too great and Macduff proclaims Malcolm unfit to even live. Answers will vary. As Christians we clearly need to demand, encourage, and exhibit the kind of leadership and rule described in these verses—conversant in and obedient to the laws of God, wise, just, temperate, etc.—but such leaders are not always available in general society. Then the truly hard choices must be made, choices such as Macduff seems to face here. We should never, however, try to appease or gloss over sin or sinful character as Macduff seems to try to do or as we so often see done in society. Acknowledging the world to be as it is and dealing with it does not mean approving of it or justifying it.

13. Answers will vary. In a sense, this question is unanswerable except as general guidelines. The passage in Daniel deals with a case in which the men were ordered to do something in direct contradiction to the laws of God and so they disobeyed the ruler. The 2 Samuel passage deals with a general who was ordered to do something that was unwise because it was against the principles of humility and trusting in God's strength and provision, and so he voiced his objection but obeyed the royal command. The Romans and 1 Peter passages direct us to obey those in authority over us because they have been put there by God. Though answers will vary, a principle seems to be that we are to obey the authorities until they command us to do something that contradicts the commands of God. As Malcolm notes, exactly where that line is drawn sometimes will be a matter of contention among Godly and well-intentioned people.

Act V

Vocabulary:

1. disturbance, confusion; 2. injure, destroy; 3. spiritual, holy; 4. remedy, something that relieves; 5. unspoiled, pure, original state; 6. cleansing, emptying; 7. forced, compelled; 8. evasion, double meaning, half-truth; 9. noisy, tumultuous; 10. one who has taken by treachery or without right

Scrambled Quotation:

Life's but a walking shadow, a poor player that struts and frets his hour upon the stage and then is heard no more.—Macbeth, Act V, scene v.

General Questions:

1. Lady Macbeth seems to be losing her mind and finally commits suicide.

2. The doctor says that "unnatural deeds do breed unnatural troubles." He implies that she has an "infected" mind, and "More needs she the divine than the physician." In other words, he can't really help her, she needs God's help. He tells the gentlewoman to watch her closely and avoid annoying or disturbing her.

3. Apparently it has become clear to all that Macbeth has gained the throne by treachery and not by legitimate or justifiable means: "He cannot buckle his distempered cause/ Within the belt of rule." People believe he is insane—some just call it fury—but apparently no one follows or obeys him willingly, only by coercion. Their words imply that he is unpredictable and harsh.

4. Malcolm tells his troops to cut limbs from the trees and carry them so Macbeth will not be able to judge their true numbers. In this way, Birnam Wood comes to Dunsinane, fulfilling the prophecy that had seemed to mean that Macbeth would never be defeated ("Macbeth shall never vanquished be until/ Great Birnam Wood to high Dunsinane Hill/ Shall come against him."). Now he realizes that the prophecy signals his defeat.

Macbeth Study Guide

5. Macduff says he was "from his mother's womb untimely ripped," he was born by cesarean section, and therefore technically not "of woman born." The Apparitions warned Macbeth to beware of Macduff, but that no one of woman born could harm him. Macbeth now realizes that his doom stands before him.

6. Many of the troops join with Malcolm and Siward. The rest seem to fight half-heartedly at best.

Analysis:

7. Answers will vary. In a strange juxtaposition, the first battle was fought to defeat a rebellion against the legitimate king, but the last battle is fought by the heir apparent to the throne to regain the throne from a murderous rebel, Macbeth. In the first battle Macbeth kills many men as he snatches victory for Duncan. In this final battle, however, Macbeth appears to defeat only a boy, though he makes great boasts and threats. The first battle is fierce and bloody, the second quick and "gentle." No one comes to the rebel king's aid, no one stands by him in the end.

8. In Act I, scene v, instead of wanting a light, Lady Macbeth cried, "Come, thick night,/ And pall thee in the dunnest smoke of hell,/ . . . Nor heaven peep through the blanket of the dark/ To cry 'Hold, hold!'" Lady Macbeth has gone from calling forth darkness to cover her actions to not being able to sleep without a light. Far from being the mistress of darkness, she now finds herself its victim. Likewise, after the murder of Duncan in Act II, scene ii, Lady Macbeth declares to her husband, "A little water clears us of this deed. How easy it is then!" She had believed that the consequences of the murder would be minimal, erased with a little water. Now she sees and smells the literal and figurative blood on her hands even in her sleep and believes nothing will take it away.

9. Answers will vary. In the line, "The Thane of Fife had a wife. Where is she now?" it is possible that Lady Macbeth is gloating over the death of Lady Macduff. However, it is also possible that Lady Macbeth knew nothing of the plans for the massacre of Macduff's family, and that the pointless murder of innocent women and children touches her unlike the killing of Duncan and Banquo; that Lady Macbeth is horrified by the killing of Macduff's wife and children and realizes that their blood also is on her hands for encouraging Macbeth to start this business. In the line, "No more o' that, my lord," she may be trying to stop Macbeth from more killing, or she may be be chiding him for weakness. "You mar all with this starting" may refer to his agitation earlier after the killing of Duncan and Banquo or may refer to his continued agitation and killing (as Macbeth said in Act IV, "From this moment the very firstlings of my heart shall be the firstlings of my hand"). Because of her mental agitation and confusion, and because many of the words have two meanings (such as *starting*), definitive answers will be difficult to give, but the possibilities are intriguing.

10. Macbeth demands that the doctor cure Lady Macbeth—fix her diseased mind, take away her trouble, cleanse her heart. The doctor replies, "Therein the patient must minister to himself." Macbeth's response, "Throw physic to the dogs. I'll none of it," demonstrates that Macbeth still wants to avoid personal responsibility. If he (or his wife) has to face what they have done, to admit their wrongs, to come to grips with their sin to achieve peace, then he wants "none of it."

11. Macbeth is saying, in essence, "If only you could figure out what's wrong with my country and cure her, I would sing your praises from the highest hills." The irony is that Macbeth himself is the disease in Scotland; everything seemed well until he murdered the king and began a rule of injustice and cruelty. This apparent blindness may mean that he truly does not see the effects of his actions, that he is so self-centered that he cannot see the horrors his actions cause.

12. Macbeth seems to be acting without thinking, repeatedly interrupting people, interrupting himself, giving contradictory directions ("Bring me no more reports," "What news more?"; "Give me my armor," "Pull 't off, I say."). He does not seem to stop and plan anything anymore, either his words or his actions.

Dig Deeper:

13. Answers will vary. It could be that he feels as secure as he claims, but the continued proclamations about his fearlessness ("I cannot taint with fear," "Fear not, Macbeth," "The mind I sway by and the heart I bear/ Shall never sag with doubt nor shake with fear," "Hang those that talk of fear," "I will not be afraid of death and bane," and more), and the continued reference to the prophecies seem to indicate that he is reassuring himself and using them to fight off a sense of impending doom. These verses reveal God's disdain for boasting and pride, they will be punished.

14. Answers will vary. There are two main interpretations of the first line; either "She should have lived longer," or "She would have died later anyway." The first interpretation implies sadness, or at least wistfulness, at her death, the second implies that Macbeth has lost love and no longer has much concern for anyone but himself. In either case, it seems a dramatic change from their earlier scenes together, in which there seemed to be an honest and actual love or connection and affection between the two. He seems to have an immense boredom with life and seems to see it as useless and insub-

Macbeth Study Guide

stantial. The repetition of *tomorrow,* the word *creeps,* "to the last syllable of recorded time," all speak of slow movement and monotony. The other imagery, "walking shadow," "poor player," "stage," "tale," speaks of emptiness and facade.

15. Answers will vary. Macbeth does not accept the conditions because he refuses to bow to Malcolm and be mocked. His pride is too great for that; perhaps he has for too long thought of himself as privileged and invincible. Macduff has already said he wants Macbeth's head. His "terms of surrender" seem to be inflammatory to get Macbeth to fight.

16. Answer will vary.

17. Siward seems concerned only with whether his son died honorably ("Had he his hurts before?") and gives him little other concern ("He's worth no more [sorrow]./ They say he parted well and paid his score,/ And so, God be with him.") Answers will vary.

Overview

1. Answers will vary.

2. The metaphor appears in Act I, scene iii, as "borrowed robes"; same scene, "New honors come upon him,/ Like our strange garments, cleave not to their mold/ But with the aid of use"; Act I, scene vii, "golden opinions . . . which would be worn now in their newest gloss"; same scene, "Was the hope drunk/ Wherein you dressed yourself?"; Act II, scene iii, "Let's briefly put on manly readiness/ And meet i' th' hall together"; Act II, scene iv, "Adieu,/ Lest our old robes sit easier than our new"; Act V, scene ii, "Now does he feel his title/ Hang loose about him, like a giant's robe/ Upon a dwarfish thief." Answers will vary. The honors that Macbeth takes for himself are not fitting to him, they are but cloth covering on the true man. He can cover himself with them, but he can never wear them as his own.

3. Answers will vary. As Christians we generally believe all men are redeemable, but within the action of this play, that need not be the case. Some points of no return may be when he understands the witches' prophecy may come true, when he writes to his wife, when he returns to his wife, after the dinner party, after he has killed Duncan, after he has killed Banquo and/or Macduff's family, after the witches' have apparently declared him invincible, after his wife's death.

4. The passages about Abraham and Jacob each have a prophecy: Abram would become a father and progenitor of a nation; Jacob would rule over his brother. In both cases, rather than allowing God to fulfill his own prophecy, the men took it upon themselves to "help" God. In Abraham's case the consequences were catastrophic and affect history to this day in the conflict between the Arabs and the Jews. In Jacob's case it meant he had to leave his home and live in fear for decades. On the other hand, Gideon was told what to do by God, and, by following God's instruction even when it didn't seem to make sense, he was able to accomplish all God had said he would. David was anointed king as a boy, and because he honored God, even when it seemed he should take matters into his own hands, God not only made him and his descendants king but also established his line forever as the line of the Messiah. The general rule is that God is able to accomplish what he says he will do, and we should not presume to take matters into our own hands.

5. Answers will vary.

6. The characters' response to death is varied and difficult to explain. Macduff is truly horrified at the death of Duncan; only he seems to give voice to honest grief. Malcolm and Donalbain seem to not feel sorrow yet ("Our tears are not yet brewed." "Nor our strong sorrow"). When Macduff learns of his family's murders, Malcolm responds, "Be comforted. Let's make us med'cines of our great revenge"—he urges revenge in place of grief. But Macduff shows honest grief: "I shall do so,/ But I must also feel it as a man./ I cannot but remember such things were/ That were most precious to me." When Lady Macbeth dies, Macbeth's response is ambiguous at best ("She should have died hereafter"). And we have dealt with the death of Siward's son in question 17 of Act V. It appears that only Macduff shows honest, heartfelt grief. Answer will vary about why people respond the way they do.

7. Answers will vary. The most likely spots for evidence of the change in Lady Macbeth's control or circumstances might be in Act III, scene ii, where Lady Macbeth says, "Naught's had, all's spent,/ Where our desire is got without content./ 'Tis safer to be that which we destroy/ Than by destruction dwell in doubtful joy"; or a little later in the same scene when she has to ask Macbeth, "What's to be done?" These are arguably the first points at which she expresses uncertainty or does not control the circumstances of their plotting. Another point may be after the deaths of Macduff's wife and children, which she refers to while sleepwalking. Accept other, reasonable answers, including answers that take issue with the premise of the question.

8. Answers will vary. Briefly, in the beginning Macbeth seems to be a hero, conquering enemies and defending his king. As soon as the title of king is dangled before him, however, he seems to be filled with a desire to have it, though he also appears quite nervous about the possible consequences. After the murder, however, and particularly after he has been

Macbeth Study Guide

crowned, he begins to act authoritatively and decisively. He no longer asks for the direction, or even advice, of his wife. He seems to begin to embrace evil ("Things bad begun make strong themselves by ill."). He determines to act only for himself: "For mine own good, All causes shall give way. I am in blood stepped in so far that, should I wade no more, returning were as tedious as go o'er. Strange things I have in head, that will to hand, which must be acted ere they may be scanned." He no longer gives thought to anyone but himself and decides not to think before he acts. At the end of the play we see the culmination of these decisions—he seems to show little remorse even at the death of his wife, and he is so much acting without thinking that he repeatedly contradicts himself to his messengers and servants. His choices have "unmanned" him—made him almost inhuman.

9. Answers will vary.

10. Answers will vary. Although in the first few scenes of Act I Macbeth looks as if he might be a classic hero, he most definitely quickly becomes a tragic hero or an antihero. Accept reasonable and well-reasoned answers. He probably does differ from classic definitions in that if he is a tragic hero he does not seem to accept responsibility for his actions even at the end, and if he is an antihero, there seems to have been good in him to begin with.

11. Both Macbeth's statements and the Ecclesiastes passages have a hopeless feel to them—joy is gone and life is monotonous or pointless. In Ephesians Paul tells us that our lives were once pointless and dead, but God has raised us up to hope and life in Jesus.

12. Macbeth is saying if by murdering Duncan he could be sure of success, he would not care about what happened to him after he died ("jump the life to come"). He is more worried that he will be called to account in this life. Most of our sins are committed because we are are thinking of our pleasure here, and often we do or don't do things based on whether we might get caught. In these verses, Paul says all the good things of this life, all accomplishments, are worthless compared to a relationship with God and living all eternity with God. He would rather die and go to be with God than continue living here, but he will continue to live his life to the glory of God for the benefit of those around him and to honor God. Although we often do not live this way, partly because eternity seems remote while our lives and desires here are immediate and tangible, clearly an eternal relationship with God is more beneficial than temporary and perishable accomplishments on earth.

13. Answers may vary. The statements foreshadow these things: <u>Banquo</u>—the witches did indeed tell partial truths that ensnared and betrayed Macbeth, led to the near destruction of Scotland, and destroyed Macbeth in the end; <u>Duncan</u>—Duncan could not tell those who would betray him, he put much faith and honor in Macbeth and Macbeth was a worse traitor than the previous Thane of Cawdor; <u>Macbeth</u>—Macbeth meant this speech to prove his love for Duncan, but it truly described what his life would be like from that moment on, his life became drudgery and lost all blessing.

14. The first measure is whether what such people say comes about. If not, then we know they are not from God. Sometimes the things they say do happen, but their words or instructions are not consistent with what the Bible says. These are not from God either. Whenever someone claims to have a message from God, whether a prediction or a teaching, their words must be compared to what God has already told us in the Bible, because God does not contradict himself or change his mind. Anyone or anything that claims to be from God but does not agree with his word is to be avoided.

15. In one sense we are without hope before God, if we try to rely on ourselves and our good works. Sin is sin. One sin violates God's law and sends us into condemnation. No one can earn his salvation. The only way to a relationship with God is by putting your faith and trust in Jesus, by accepting his death as payment for your sins. Note that God has repeatedly forgiven the deepest kinds of sin—King David's adultery and the murder he stages are examples (2 Samuel 11 and 12).

© 2000 Progeny Press

Macbeth Study Guide

Suggestions for Further Reading

Other plays by William Shakespeare:

Tragedy:
Romeo and Juliet
Othello
King Lear
Hamlet

Historical Plays:
Henry IV (parts I and II)
Henry V
Julius Caesar

Comedy:
As You Like It
All's Well That Ends Well
The Merchant of Venice
A Midsummer-Night's Dream
The Taming of the Shrew

Books about Shakespeare:

Bard of Avon: the Story of William Shakespeare — by Diane Stanley, grades 7 & up, published by Morrow

Shakespeare's Life and Times — by Roland Mushat Frye, grades 9 & up

Prefaces to Shakespeare — by Harley Granville-Barker, grades 10 & up

Essays on Shakespeare — edited by Gerald W. Chapman, grades 10 & up

Videos:

Macbeth — 1983, British Broadcasting Company, directed by Jack Gold

Macbeth — 1948, directed by and starring Orson Welles. (*Note:* this film deviated from the text and was melodramatic.)

Hamlet — 1990, Warner Brothers, starring Mel Gibson and Glenn Close

Much Ado About Nothing — 1993, starring Kenneth Branagh and Emma Thompson.

Henry V — 1990, CBS/Fox, starring Kenneth Branagh

Romeo and Juliet — 1968, starring Leonard Whiting, Olivia Hussey, Milo O'Shea, and Michael York

Study Guides Available from Progeny Press

Visit our website and online store for a complete listing of our study guides.

Lower Elementary
*Prereader Study Guide: Oscar Otter and
Henry & Mudge in Puddle Trouble
The Bears on Hemlock Mountain
Clipper Ship
The Courage of Sarah Noble
The Drinking Gourd
Frog and Toad Together
The Josefina Story Quilt
Keep the Lights Burning, Abbie
The Long Way to a New Land
The Long Way Westward
The Minstrel in the Tower
Miss Rumphius
A New Coat for Anna
Ox-Cart Man
Sam the Minuteman
Wagon Wheels*

Upper Elementary
*The Best Christmas Pageant Ever
The Bridge
Charlotte's Web
The Cricket in Times Square
Crown and Jewel
The Door in the Wall
Farmer Boy
In the Year of the Boar and Jackie Robinson
Little House in the Big Woods
Little House on the Prairie
Sarah, Plain and Tall
The Two Collars
The Whipping Boy*

Middle School
*The Adventures of Tom Sawyer
Amos Fortune, Free Man
Anne of Green Gables
Bridge to Terabithia
The Bronze Bow
Carry On, Mr. Bowditch
The Giver
The Hiding Place
Holes
The Indian in the Cupboard
Island of the Blue Dolphins*

*Johnny Tremain
The Lion, the Witch and the Wardrobe
The Magician's Nephew
Maniac Magee
Number the Stars
Out of the Dust
Prince Caspian
Redwall
Roll of Thunder, Hear My Cry
The Secret Garden
Shiloh
The Sign of the Beaver
Tuck Everlasting
Where the Red Fern Grows
The Witch of Blackbird Pond
A Wrinkle in Time*

High School
*The Adventures of Huckleberry Finn
A Christmas Carol
A Day No Pigs Would Die
Frankenstein
The Great Gatsby
Hamlet
Heart of Darkness
The Hobbit
Introduction to Poetry: Forms and Elements
Jane Eyre
Lord of the Flies
The Lord of the Rings: The Fellowship of the Ring
The Lord of the Rings: The Two Towers
The Lord of the Rings: The Return of the King
Macbeth
The Merchant of Venice
The Old Man and the Sea
Out of the Silent Planet
Perelandra
The Red Badge of Courage
Romeo and Juliet
The Scarlet Letter
The Screwtape Letters
The Strange Case of Dr. Jekyll and Mr. Hyde
The Swiss Family Robinson
A Tale of Two Cities
To Kill a Mockingbird
The Yearling*

www.progenypress.com

1-877-PROGENY   progeny@progenypress.com